FUN WITH CHINESE HOROSCOPES

written and illustrated
by evelyn lip

Published by
**Graham Brash (Pte) Ltd
Singapore.**

Dedicated to:

By:

Preface

Much has been written about Chinese Horoscopes, but the subject has rarely been presented in the form of light-hearted cartoons. In this book, the characteristics and idiosyncrasies of those born under each of the animal symbols are illustrated in over one hundred and thirty sketches which will entertain and delight the reader.

Introduction

The twelve Animal Symbols correspond with the "Twelve Branches", as follows:

Animal	Branch
Rat	Zi
Ox	Chou
Tiger	Yin
Rabbit	Mao
Dragon	Chen
Snake	Si
Horse	Wu
Goat	Wei
Monkey	Shen
Rooster	You
Dog	Shu
Pig	Hai

They existed in folk tradition as far back as the 6th century B.C., but it was not until the 3rd century B.C. that Huang Ti (Emperor of China) initiated the formal study of astronomy and astrology, and that the lunar calender was devised.

Each lunar year is represented by one of the twelve animal symbols, and the common belief is that a person has characteristics similar to those of the animal which rules the year of his birth. To quote Li Hai Chi (蠡海集) of the Sung Dynasty, "Man is associated with the Animal Symbols and the Branches ...... for the father confers the essence of life .... "

It is hoped that the reader will have fun finding out more about himself, acknowledging the virtues and disclaiming the vices attributed to him by his Chinese Horoscope.

Calender Chart

DATE OF BIRTH	ANIMAL	DATE OF BIRTH	ANIMAL
12.2.1888 — 30.1.1889	Rat	24.1.1936 — 10.2.1937	Rat
31.1.1889 — 20.1.1890	Ox	11.2.1937 — 30.1.1938	Ox
21.1.1890 — 8.2.1891	Tiger	31.1.1938 — 18.2.1939	Tiger
9.2.1891 — 29.1.1892	Rabbit	19.2.1939 — 7.2.1940	Rabbit
30.1.1892 — 16.2.1893	Dragon	8.2.1940 — 26.1.1941	Dragon
17.2.1893 — 5.2.1894	Snake	27.1.1941 — 14.2.1942	Snake
6.2.1894 — 25.1.1895	Horse	15.2.1942 — 4.2.1943	Horse
26.1.1895 — 12.2.1896	Goat	5.2.1943 — 24.1.1944	Goat
13.2.1896 — 1.2.1897	Monkey	25.1.1944 — 12.2.1945	Monkey
2.2.1897 — 21.1.1898	Rooster	13.2.1945 — 1.2.1946	Rooster
22.1.1898 — 9.2.1899	Dog	2.2.1946 — 21.1.1947	Dog
10.2.1899 — 31.1.1900	Pig	22.1.1947 — 9.2.1948	Pig
1.2.1900 — 18.2.1901	Rat	10.2.1948 — 28.1.1949	Rat
19.2.1901 — 7.2.1902	Ox	29.1.1949 — 16.2.1950	Ox
8.2.1902 — 28.1.1903	Tiger	17.2.1950 — 5.2.1951	Tiger
29.1.1903 — 15.2.1904	Rabbit	6.2.1951 — 26.1.1952	Rabbit
16.2.1904 — 3.2.1905	Dragon	27.1.1952 — 13.2.1953	Dragon
4.2.1905 — 24.1.1906	Snake	14.2.1953 — 2.2.1954	Snake
25.1.1906 — 12.2.1907	Horse	3.2.1954 — 23.1.1955	Horse
13.2.1907 — 1.2.1908	Goat	26.1.1955 — 11.2.1956	Goat
2.2.1908 — 21.1.1909	Monkey	12.2.1956 — 30.1.1957	Monkey
22.1.1909 — 9.2.1910	Rooster	31.1.1957 — 17.2.1958	Rooster
10.2.1910 — 29.1.1911	Dog	18.2.1958 — 7.2.1959	Dog
30.1.1911 — 17.2.1912	Pig	8.2.1959 — 27.1.1960	Pig
18.2.1912 — 5.2.1913	Rat	28.1.1960 — 14.2.1961	Rat
6.2.1913 — 25.1.1914	Ox	15.2.1961 — 4.2.1962	Ox
26.1.1914 — 13.2.1915	Tiger	5.2.1962 — 24.1.1963	Tiger
14.2.1915 — 3.2.1916	Rabbit	25.1.1963 — 12.2.1964	Rabbit
4.2.1916 — 22.1.1917	Dragon	13.2.1964 — 1.2.1965	Dragon
23.1.1917 — 10.2.1918	Snake	2.2.1965 — 20.1.1966	Snake
11.2.1918 — 31.1.1919	Horse	21.1.1966 — 8.2.1967	Horse
1.2.1919 — 19.2.1920	Goat	9.2.1967 — 29.1.1968	Goat
20.2.1920 — 7.2.1921	Monkey	30.1.1968 — 16.2.1969	Monkey
8.2.1921 — 27.1.1922	Rooster	17.2.1969 — 5.2.1970	Rooster
28.1.1922 — 15.2.1923	Dog	6.2.1970 — 26.1.1971	Dog
16.2.1923 — 4.2.1924	Pig	27.1.1971 — 14.2.1972	Pig
5.2.1924 — 23.1.1925	Rat	15.2.1972 — 2.2.1973	Rat
24.1.1925 — 12.2.1926	Ox	3.2.1973 — 22.1.1974	Ox
13.2.1926 — 1.2.1927	Tiger	23.1.1974 — 10.2.1975	Tiger
2.2.1927 — 22.1.1928	Rabbit	11.2.1975 — 30.1.1976	Rabbit
23.1.1928 — 9.2.1929	Dragon	31.1.1976 — 17.2.1977	Dragon
10.2.1929 — 29.1.1930	Snake	18.2.1977 — 6.2.1978	Snake
30.1.1930 — 16.2.1931	Horse	7.2.1978 — 27.1.1979	Horse
17.2.1931 — 5.2.1932	Goat	28.1.1979 — 15.2.1980	Goat
6.2.1932 — 25.1.1933	Monkey	16.2.1980 — 4.2.1981	Monkey
26.1.1933 — 13.2.1934	Rooster	5.2.1981 — 24.1.1982	Rooster
14.2.1934 — 3.2.1935	Dog	25.1.1982 — 12.2.1983	Dog
4.2.1935 — 23.1.1936	Pig	13.2.1983 — 1.2.1984	Pig

ARE YOU A DOG, A HORSE OR A RAT?
ARE YOU AN INTROVERT OR EXTROVERT?
ARE YOU A PRACTICAL OR IMPRACTICAL
PERSON?

IT DEPENDS ON YOUR YEAR OF BIRTH.

THE CHART ON PAGE 6 WILL TELL YOU
TO WHICH ANIMAL SYMBOL YOU
BELONG.

THE SKETCHES IN THE BOOK ILLUS-
TRATE SOME OF THE CHARACTERIS-
TICS OF EACH ANIMAL SYMBOL.

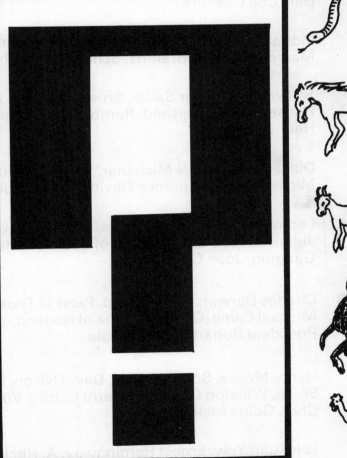

7

Some Outstanding Personalities

RAT: Tchaikovsky, William Shakespeare, Marlon Brando, Doris Day, Leo Tolstoy, Mozart, Jimmy Carter, Prince Charles.

OX: Walt Disney, Rubens, Emperor Hirohito, Hitler, J. Fonda, S. Bassey, Nehru, Napoleon Bonarparte, Margaret Thatcher.

TIGER: Charles de Gaulle, Dwight Eisenhower, Karl Marx, Queen Elizabeth II, Ho Chi Minh, Beethoven, Marilyn Monroe, Giscard D'Estaing, Rudolf Nureyev.

RABBIT: Bob Hope, Fidel Castro, Martin Luther King, Einstein, Stalin, King Bhumibol, Queen Victoria, David Frost, Ali McGraw.

DRAGON: Emperor Ch'ien Lung, Joan of Arc, Picasso, John Lennon, Yehudi Menuhin, Abraham Lincoln, Frank Sinatra, Salvador Dali, Che Guevara.

SNAKE: Indira Gandhi, John Kennedy, Mao Tse-tung, Liszt, Ferdinand Marcos, Picasso, Brahms, Schubert, Abraham Lincoln.

HORSE: Stravinsky, Anwar Sadat, Krushchev, Neil Armstrong, Roosevelt, B. Streisand, Rembrandt, Raquel Welsh, Brezhnev, Helmut Schmidt.

GOAT: Diana Dors, James Michener, Liberace, Muhammad Ali, Michelangelo, Laurence Olivier, Pierre Trudeau, Takeo Miki.

MONKEY: Leonardo da Vinci, Descartes, Charles Dickens, John Milton, Julius Caesar, Queen Sirikit of Thailand, Harry Truman, Gauguin, Joan Crawford.

ROOSTER: Charles Darwin, Prince Philip, Peter O'Toole, Andrei Gromyko, Michael Caine, Queen Juliana of Holland, Yves Montand, President Suharto of Indonesia.

DOG: Henry Moore, Sophia Loren, David Niven, R. Hakluyt, Chou En-lai, Winston Churchill, Pierre Cardin, Voltaire, Elvis Presley, Cher, Golda Meir.

PIG: Lee Kuan Yew, Ernest Hemingway, A. Hitchcock, J. Mathis, G. Pompidou, John D. Rockefeller, Ronald Reagan, Maria Callas, King Hussein of Jordan, Francoise Sagan, H. Kissinger.

Contents

Contents

The Rat

If born in one of the following periods:

12th February 1888 to 30th January 1889
1st February 1900 to 18th February 1901
18th February 1912 to 5th February 1913
5th February 1924 to 23rd January 1925
24th January 1936 to 10th February 1937
10th February 1948 to 28th January 1949
28th January 1960 to 14th February 1961
15th February 1972 to 2nd February 1973
2nd February 1984 to 19th February 1985

You are a Rat

A person born during the year of the Rat is normally very generous but can be rather petty.

He is generally intelligent and hard working but can at times be extremely idle.

12

He has many friends but few are close or loyal to him.

He saves and is thrifty but when he is in the mood, he spends generously.

He may be very successful, yet he feels insecure.

He is usually diplomatic, but at times he can be critical or perverse to the point of being unfair.

He aims high and loves a challenge.

He is a persuasive speaker and can be a good businessman or politician.

He woos you with extravagant gifts and attention.

He tends to get into emotional entanglements.

He is best suited to the Dragon, Monkey and Ox but does not get on with the Horse and Rabbit.

The Ox

If born in one of the following periods:

31st January 1889 to 20th January 1890
19th February 1901 to 7th February 1902
6th February 1913 to 25th January 1914
24th January 1925 to 12th February 1926
11th February 1937 to 30th January 1938
29th January 1949 to 16th February 1950
15th February 1961 to 4th February 1962
3rd February 1973 to 22nd January 1974
20th February 1985 to 8th February 1986

You are an Ox

He is challenging the rocks.

A person born under the Ox sign is superbly healthy .... and magnificently obstinate.

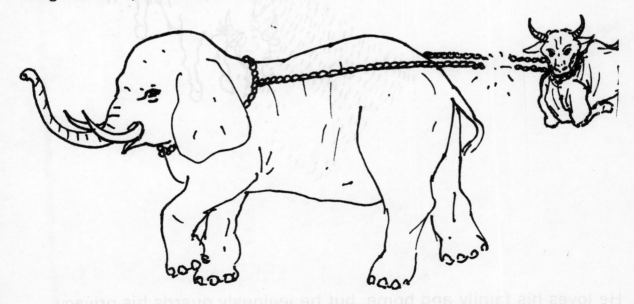

Once he has made up his mind, nothing can move him.

He loves his family and home, but he jealously guards his privacy and independence.

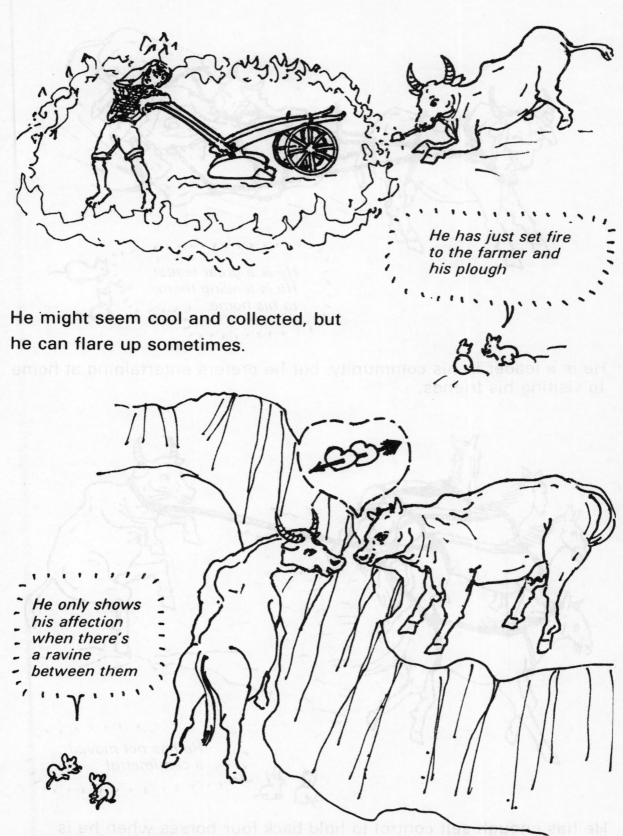

He has just set fire to the farmer and his plough

He might seem cool and collected, but he can flare up sometimes.

He only shows his affection when there's a ravine between them

He is attracted to the opposite sex, but is shy and conservative.

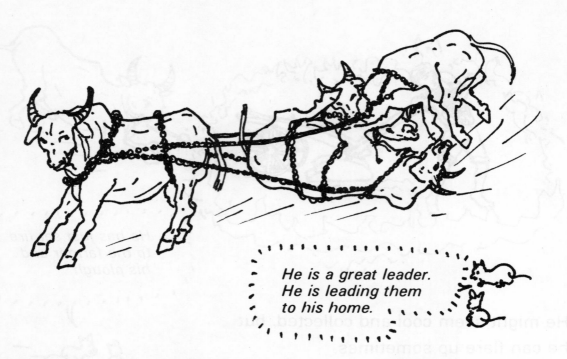

He is a great leader.
He is leading them
to his home.

He is a leader in his community, but he prefers entertaining at home to visiting his friends.

He has not moved
a centimetre!

He has enough self control to hold back four horses when he is determined.

He loves outdoor life and old fashioned things.

He may rush to a sale but not into courtship.

23

He sticks to anything he starts and always finishes what he begins.

His compatible marriage partners are the Snake, the Rat or the Rooster. His opposing symbols are the Tiger, the Goat and the Monkey.

The Tiger

If born in one of the following periods:

21st January 1890 to 8th February 1891
8th February 1902 to 28th January 1903
26th January 1914 to 13th February 1915
13th February 1926 to 1st February 1927
31st January 1938 to 18th February 1939
17th February 1950 to 5th February 1951
5th February 1962 to 24th January 1963
23rd January 1974 to 10th February 1975
9th February 1986 to 28th February 1987

You are a Tiger

A person born during the year of the Tiger is adventurous and daring.

He is idealistic and creative.

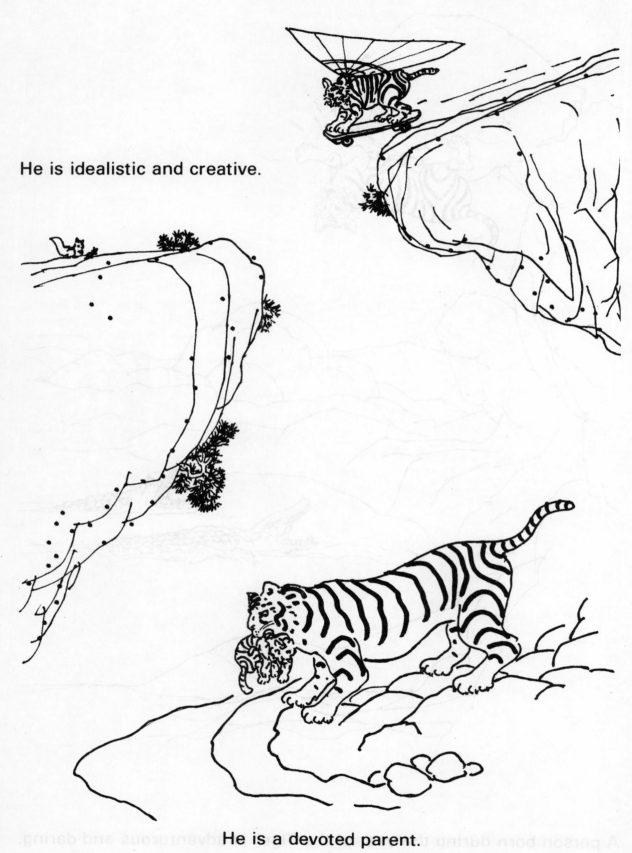

He is a devoted parent.

He is confident. Even though he falls down he gets up and tries again.

He has contagious enthusiasm and a magnetic personality.

He fears nothing and no one — until he gets burned.

Despite his forwardness he can be diplomatic and sustain social grace.

Being a realist, he enjoys opposition and overcomes obstacles with confidence.

Being practical, he can be successful in business.

He is a pioneer and always aims at impossible goals.

He is most suited to the Horse as marriage partner. The Dragon, Pig and Dog are also compatible.

He must avoid the Snake and Monkey.

The Rabbit

If born in one of the following periods:

9th February 1891 to 29th January 1892
29th January 1903 to 15th February 1904
14th February 1915 to 3rd February 1916
2nd February 1927 to 22nd January 1928
19th February 1939 to 7th February 1940
6th February 1951 to 26th January 1952
25th January 1963 to 12th February 1964
11th February 1975 to 30th January 1976
29th February 1987 to 16th February 1988

You are a Rabbit

A person born during the year of the Rabbit is peace loving and elegant.

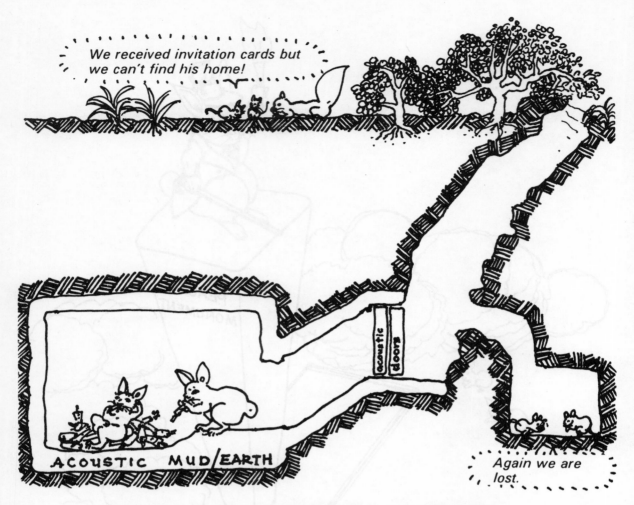

He is sociable, yet he loves a quiet life style.

He is unselfishly devoted to his family and friends.

He tends to be timid.

They are hungry. They'll pay anything for the carrots.

Very often he is a good business man.

He is easily upset and disturbed. Thus he needs constant reassurance and signs of affection.

He may be a mixture of virtue and vanity.

He will sacrifice himself for his loved ones.

They have hundreds
of great grand
children.

The Rabbit is the emblem of longevity.

He is compatible with the Pig, the Dog and the Goat. The Rat, the Tiger and the Rooster are not his best friends.

The Dragon

If born in one of the following periods:

30th January 1892 to 16th February 1893
16th February 1904 to 3rd February 1905
4th February 1916 to 22nd January 1917
23rd January 1928 to 9th February 1929
8th February 1940 to 26th January 1941
27th January 1952 to 13th February 1953
13th February 1964 to 1st February 1965
31st January 1976 to 17th February 1977

You are a Dragon

A person born under the sign of the Dragon possesses a commanding air and stately bearing.

He is strong and full of vitality.

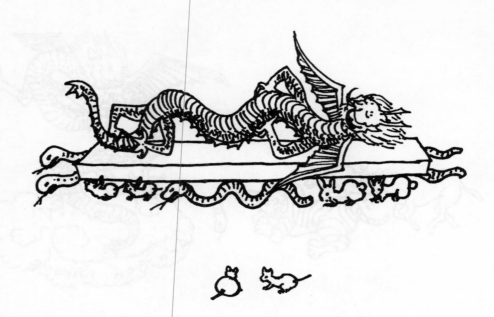

He is the social leader of his group, lording it over lesser companions.

He is popular and is often the life and soul of a party.

Being idealistic, he is difficult to please.

He is athletic and good at sports.

He is a chivalrous and gallant suitor.

He is gifted and intelligent.

He feels himself above the law and does not always practise what he preaches.

The 'lady' Dragon is a strong supporter of equal rights for women. What a man can do, she can probably do better.

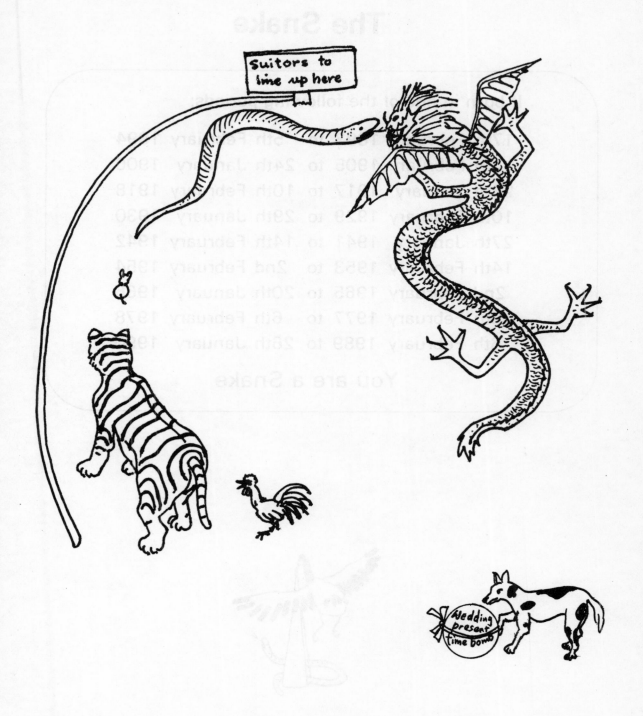

The Dragon is suited to the Snake, Rat, Monkey, Tiger and
Rooster, but not the Dog.

The Snake

If born in one of the following periods:

17th February 1893 to   5th February 1894
4th February 1905 to 24th January 1906
23rd January 1917 to 10th February 1918
10th February 1929 to 29th January 1930
27th January 1941 to 14th February 1942
14th February 1953 to   2nd February 1954
2nd February 1965 to 20th January 1966
18th February 1977 to   6th February 1978
6th February 1989 to 26th January 1990

You are a Snake

Look! Even his master can't resist his charm.

A person born during the year of the Snake has a charming personality.

He is fiercely possessive of what he owns.

For his own unfathomable reasons, he is selfish.

He is contemptuous of those whom he considers less intelligent than himself.

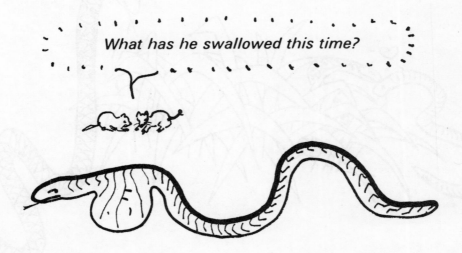

What has he swallowed this time?

He treasures his privacy, and will keep many a dark secret locked up within him.

He has a disconcerting sense of humour.

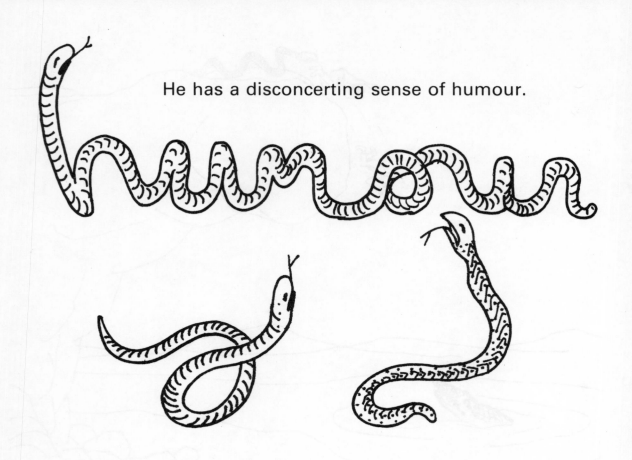

He loves mystery and is inquisitive.

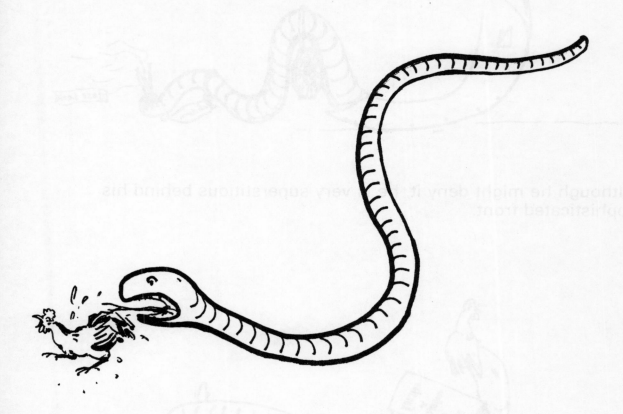

He has no qualms about eliminating anyone who stands in his way.

Although he might deny it, he is very superstitious behind his sophisticated front.

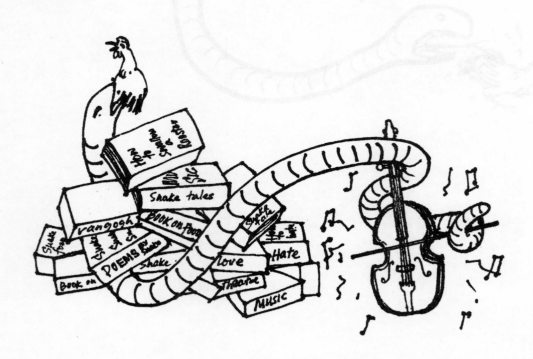

Graceful and soft-spoken, he loves good books, food, music, the theatre; he will gravitate towards all the finer things in life.

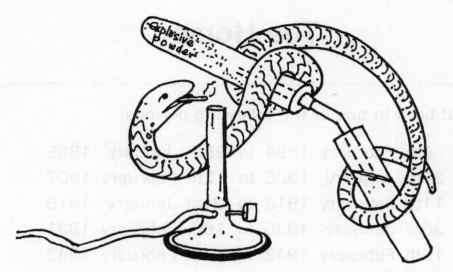

Scientist and theologian, he is a deep thinker.

His compatible marriage partners are the Dragon, Rooster and Ox while his incompatible partners are a fellow Snake, the Pig and Tiger.

The Horse

If born in one of the following periods:

6th February 1894 to 25th January 1895
28th January 1906 to 12th February 1907
11th February 1918 to 31st January 1919
30th January 1930 to 16th February 1931
15th February 1942 to 4th February 1943
3rd February 1954 to 23rd January 1955
21st January 1966 to 8th February 1967
7th February 1978 to 27th January 1979
27th January 1990 to 14th February 1991

You are a Horse

A person born under the sign of the Horse has an excellent build and a charming appearance.

He is extremely good with his hands.

He responds to high ideals and is very ambitious.

He loves humour and is quick-witted.

He is a showy dresser, partial to bright colours and striking designs.

Always analyzing situations and handling financial matters with skill, he can be a good banker and business man.

He is gracious and gentle with the young and weak.

Possessing a happy-go-lucky nature, he loves out-door sports and activities.

Statue of Love

Isn't he adorable?

Having plenty of sex-appeal and a good sense of humour, he is most popular.

He is not good at bottling up his feelings.

The horse can be a fickle soul. He falls in and out of love with equal ease.

He is a non-conformist.

His motto is "Freedom and Joy".

He is best suited to the Tiger, the Dog and the Goat. The Rat and his fellow Horse are incompatible with him.

The Goat

If born in one of the following periods:

26th January 1895 to 12th February 1896
13th February 1907 to   1st February 1908
1st February 1919 to 19th February 1920
12th February 1931 to   5th February 1932
5th February 1943 to 24th January 1944
26th January 1955 to 11th February 1956
9th February 1967 to 29th January 1968
28th January 1979 to 15th February 1980
15th February 1991 to   3rd February 1992

You are a Goat

The Goat is a charmer.

Look! They are completely under his spell.

He can charm a bird right out of its nest.

He is hesitant in his decisions.

He is rather fond of complaining.

He is very interested in the supernatural and in mythology.

Very often he is born with a silver spoon in his mouth and he has the good fortune to live on his inheritance.

In choosing a marriage partner, he puts wealth before intelligence.

He has little sense of time, so don't expect him to be punctual.

The 'lady' Goat likes dainty things, frills and trimmings.

The Goat is best suited to the Horse, the Pig and the Rabbit. The Ox and Dog are incompatible with him.

The Monkey

If born in one of the following periods:

13th February 1896 to   1st February 1897
2nd February 1908 to 21st January 1909
20th February 1920 to   7th February 1921
6th February 1932 to 25th January 1933
25th January 1944 to 12th February 1945
12th February 1956 to 30th January 1957
30th January 1968 to 16th February 1969
16th February 1980 to   4th February 1981
4th February 1992 to 22nd January 1993

You are a Monkey

A person born in the year of the Monkey is most intelligent and alert.

He has a many-faceted personality.

He can be egoistic and has high standards.

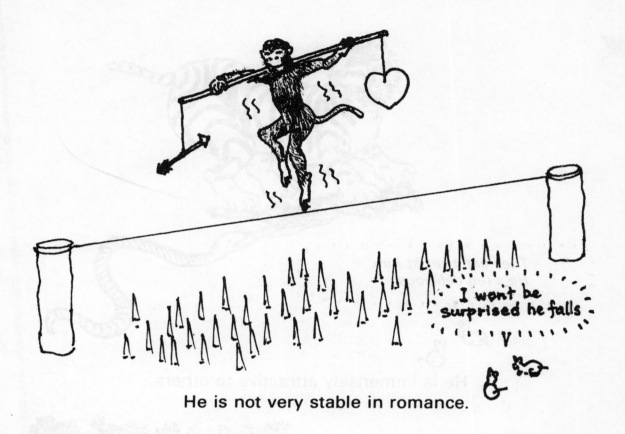

He is not very stable in romance.

He is cheeky, daring and confident.

They can't resist him.
He's too delicious.

He is immensely attractive to others.

He is an opportunist.

He is an inventor and innovator.

He can get out of any tricky situation.

He has no respect for others.

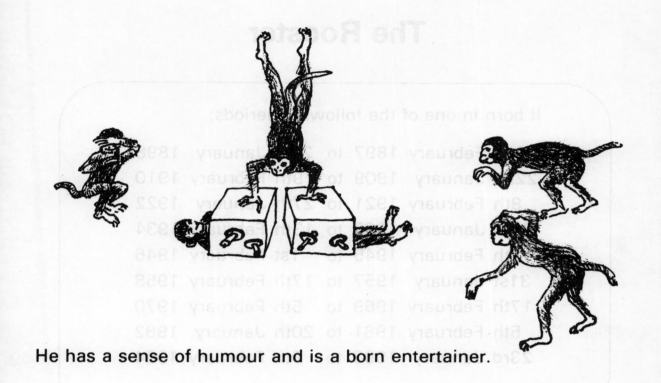

He has a sense of humour and is a born entertainer.

He gets along well with the Dragon and the Rat, but not so well with the Tiger or the Ox.

The Rooster

If born in one of the following periods:

2nd February	1897	to	21st January	1898
22nd January	1909	to	9th February	1910
8th February	1921	to	27th January	1922
26th January	1933	to	13th February	1934
13th February	1945	to	1st February	1946
31st January	1957	to	17th February	1958
17th February	1969	to	5th February	1970
5th February	1981	to	20th January	1982
23rd January	1993	to	9th February	1994

You are a Rooster

A person born during the year of the Rooster is frank, to the point of being tactless.

He may seem reckless, but he is conservative at heart.

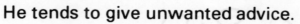

He tends to give unwanted advice.

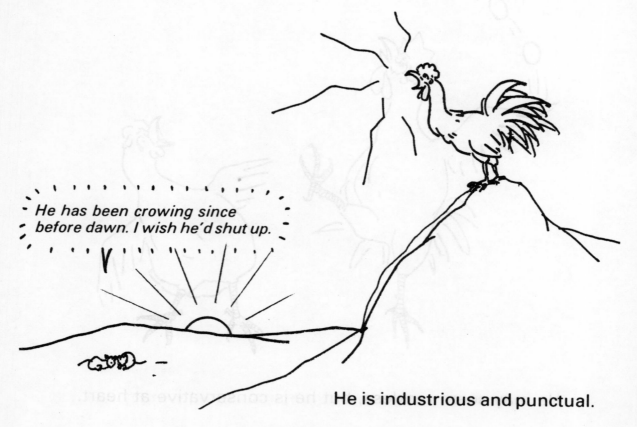

He is industrious and punctual.

Sometimes he promises more than he can give.

The 'lady' Rooster is a conscientious and meticulous worker.

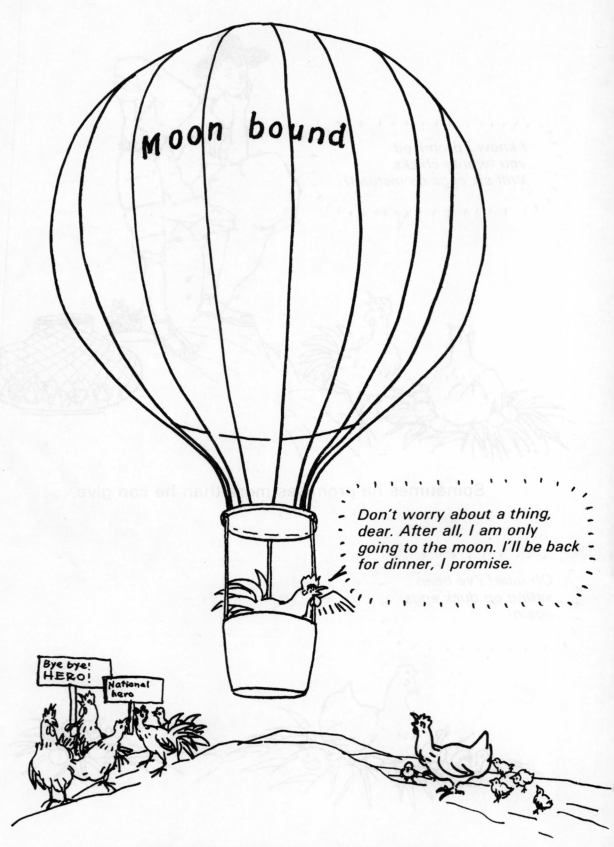

He is imaginative and dreams of being a hero or a star.

To the Rooster life is a circus or a stage. He loves to be noticed.

The emotions of the Rooster swing high and low.

His compatible marriage partners are the Snake, Dragon and Ox.

His incompatible partners are the Pig, Rabbit and a fellow Rooster.

The Dog

If born in one of the following periods:

22nd January 1898 to 9th February 1899
10th February 1910 to 29th January 1911
28th January 1922 to 15th February 1923
14th February 1934 to 3rd February 1935
2nd February 1946 to 21st January 1947
18th February 1958 to 7th February 1959
6th February 1970 to 26th January 1971
25th January 1982 to 12th February 1983
10th January 1994 to 30th January 1995

You are a Dog

A person born in the year of
the Dog is alert and watchful.

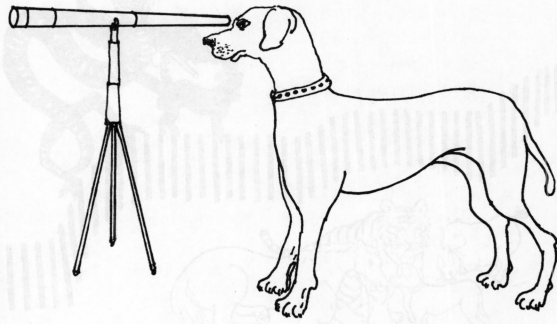

He tends to be on the defensive.

To him, everything is black or white,
everyone is a friend or an enemy.

He can be overwhelmingly generous.

He is an excellent guardian and has a strong sense of responsibility.

He is a good and patient listener.

93

He is a good organiser.

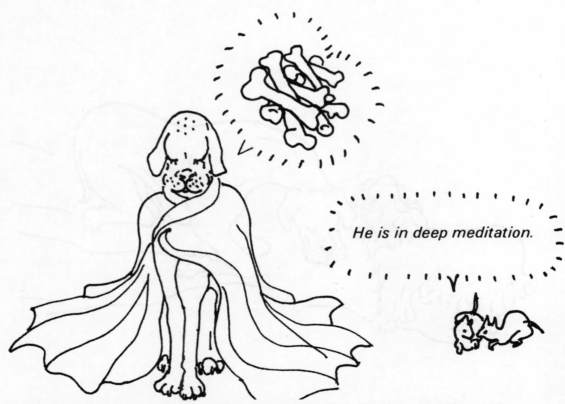

He is in deep meditation.

He is deeply spiritual and cares little for material gains.

To the Dog, family and home will always come first.

His compatible partners are the Rabbit, Pig, Tiger and Horse. The Dragon and Goat are not his best friends.

The Pig

If born in one of the following periods:

10th February 1899 to 31st January 1900
30th January 1911 to 17th February 1912
16th February 1923 to 4th February 1924
4th February 1935 to 23rd January 1936
22nd January 1947 to 9th February 1948
8th February 1959 to 27th January 1960
27th January 1971 to 14th February 1972
13th February 1983 to 1st February 1984

You are a Pig

A person born in the year of the Pig is often vulnerable.

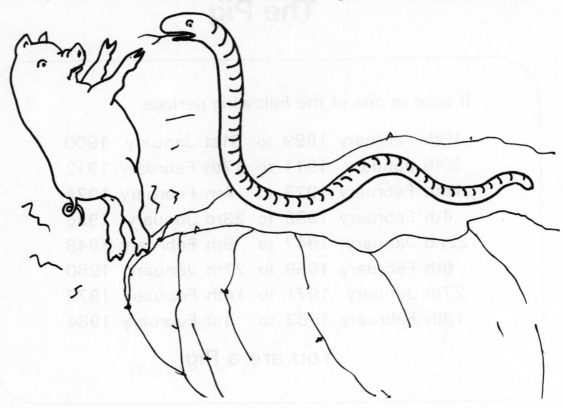

He is sometimes too honest for his own good..... and others'!

Why must Mr. Pig tell Big Wolf where he can find his children?
Can't he tell a lie!

He is materialistic and ambitious,

but is poor in handling financial matters, being more suited to literature and the arts.

Happy and gregarious, he is a good entertainer.

Being outspoken, he may tread on a few toes occasionally.

Ha ha! My wife has given
birth to a goat, two dogs and
two piglets!

Naive and pure in heart, he believes in miracles — and so miracles
will happen for him.

Because he is so kind and obliging, others tend to take advantage of him.

Calm and understanding, the Pig is a genial fellow who will tolerate a lot of nonsense from others.

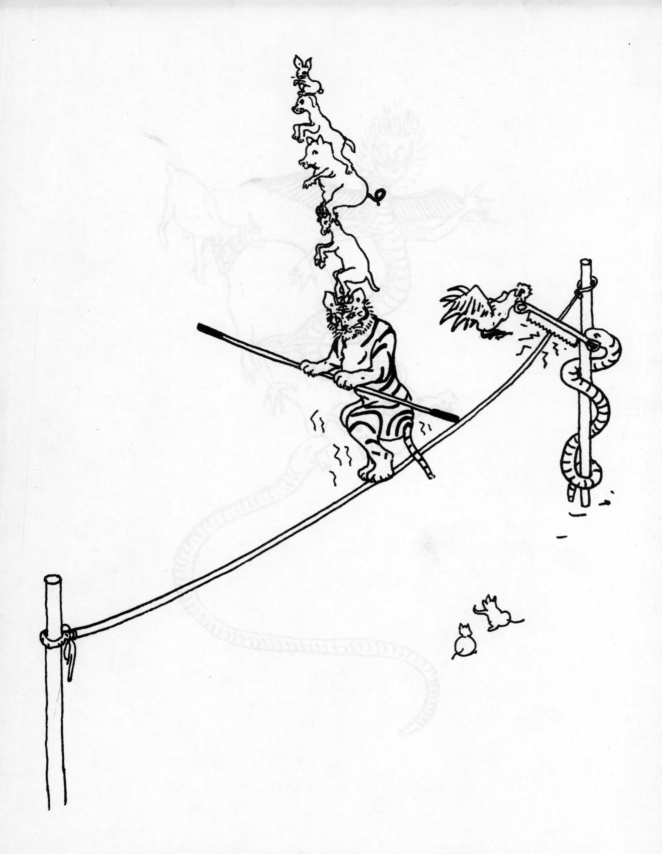

He is compatible with the Dog, Goat, Tiger and Rabbit, but not the Snake and Rooster.